Letters to
Ian

JANET GILSON

I hope you find this book comforting

Janet

Dedicated to my darling son Ian, who could not stay here with us but who is loved beyond measure and remains in my heart forever. There will always be a piece of my heart that belongs only to him.

And to my daughters, Rebecca and Sarah, without whom I wouldn't have found the strength to heal as I did and whose love continues to sustain me.

Ian Stephen Gilson born sleeping - 6th July 2002 at 7.20pm, 21 weeks.

Weighing 200 grams

"There is no foot too small, that it cannot leave an imprint on this world."

Author unknown.

TRIGGER WARNING: Contains reference to stillbirth that some may find distressing.

TABLE OF CONTENTS

Foreword

Whenever I'm asked why I chose to become a midwife, my first thought will always be Ian. Depending on the context and who I'm speaking to, I have been very selective over the years as to who gets the full story and who will get more of a broad and less personal version of events.

The book you are holding is a story of a family, my family, who had their world rocked to the core in 2002. It is not an easy story to tell, and it is only now twenty-one years later that we are all more comfortable to say his name and talk about his short but very significant presence in all of our lives. At the tender age of thirteen, I contemplated becoming a midwife. Embarking into midwifery at eighteen, I was well aware that not every family I met will go home with a baby in their arms, and that some will unfortunately leave our care with a baby in their hearts and a newly found large void in their hearts. I hoped that it may just be the little things I would do or say while caring for them that could make a large impact in how they navigate life after baby loss. My first teachers for this, as in most other aspects of one's life, were my parents, and to them I will be forever grateful. They are not perfect, but they have strived through these difficult times, with great love towards the family; me, my sister and the brother we unfortunately never had the opportunity to meet but will always hold dearly in our hearts.

~ Written by Ian's sister, Becky, in 2023

Introduction

You can never be prepared for such devastating news. Although you may have heard stories of other people who have been through the same or similar traumas, you never ever expect it to happen to you.

There is no doubt that miscarriage is extremely painful and deals its own devastating blow, especially in the case of recurring miscarriages, but the utter raw pain of holding a dead baby is beyond belief. Only those that have experienced this agonising pain can even begin to imagine how it feels and how it ultimately affects you.

The death of a baby leaves you with an overwhelming sense of loss; the loss of what might have been. How would my child have grown? What would his first words have been? How old would he have been when he took his first steps? What would his smile have looked like? What would his future have looked like? The list goes on and on, it's endless.

As the doctor/obstetrician utters the words, *"I'm sorry there seems to be a problem…"* You hope against all hope that the *"problem"* can be solved. Surely in this day and age, with all the medical advances, something can be done about the *problem*? The slow realisation that in fact nothing can be done, that they cannot find a heartbeat, or that your baby is slowly dying, brings such pain to your heart and a sickness in the pit of your stomach that just doesn't go away. The handling of such a situation should be extremely sensitive, but sadly as I know only too well, this is not always the case.

At my six-week post-delivery follow up appointment with the same obstetrician that had admitted me to hospital, he had actually dealt with the situation extremely well at that time, continued to tell me, I believe in an effort to convince me that it was better that this had happened, it's better than having a disabled or Down's syndrome child (those were his words). Whilst I wouldn't want my baby boy to suffer in any way whatsoever, it really wasn't what I needed to hear at that time when my heart was completely shattered; everything was still so real and raw. With retrospect, it is now easier to understand what he had meant. Although it is still unacceptable, he definitely shouldn't have uttered those words just six weeks after such a devastating loss.

During the initial grieving process for the son I would never get to watch grow up, I listened to a lot of other mothers who were also recovering from losses the same or similar to mine. It was during the time we had spent at a local support group where we began our healing process. One of these mothers was saddened by the fact that she would never get to write a letter to her son. This small thing really hurt me, being the prolific writer that I am, it really hit home. I had after all written many things to my daughters over the years. But wait, "*Why ever not?*" I thought, and I started to write letters to my darling son, Ian. It made me feel that I was still connected to him and helped me enormously. It gave me back the connection that I had longed for. Whenever I was thinking of him, or whenever something major was happening within our family, I would write to him to tell him and that made me feel that I could at least communicate my thoughts and feelings with him. It was just my way of including him in everything that happened.

Keeping these letters to myself was special, it was something I felt was just ours – mine and Ian's – but now it's time to share them with the rest of the World. So, I share these letters here and my thoughts on the situation I found myself in to help others who have suffered the loss of a baby. I do this in the hope that in some small way it may help, whether you got to hold and see your baby or not. If writing to your baby will help you to pour out your feelings on paper, then I believe it may be cathartic for you as it was, and still is, for me and may help as much as it has helped me.

No parent should have the pain of burying their child, and this book is also dedicated to them.

How it All Began…

My life was complete, I thought, but as I approached forty, I realised that I had a very strong yearning to add to our family. Not because I wanted a boy, as some so wrongly assumed since we already had two girls, but just because I wanted another baby to join our little family, irrespective of gender. My girls were growing up and maybe I felt that I was becoming redundant; of course, I wasn't, but still part of me longed for another child. Just before I was forty, I had an early miscarriage. It hadn't been planned but it reignited that longing for another baby. I felt that this was now my last chance. My biological clock was ticking, but it wasn't meant to be, and I had to accept, eventually, that it just wasn't part of my journey. I was blessed with my daughters and for that I will always be extremely grateful.

I feel that I had been lulled into a false sense of security seeing others having babies later in life; some of whom were famous celebrities. I mistakenly thought that this was possible for me too, even the 'norm'. I now know that at that time it was more the exception than the 'norm'. Maybe I should have been satisfied with my life and what I had and not wanted or craved for more, but I did - you can't help how you feel.

My life was full and happy. I was content, but loving babies as much as I do, I decided the time was right to have another child to add to our little clan. Following an early miscarriage, which was sad enough, I became pregnant again. I was forty-one years old and so realised I was considered high risk. However, after passing the twelve-week milestone, I then became hopeful that all would be well. In fact, I was convinced that it would be plain sailing from here on in. We then told the girls, who were excitedly looking forward to welcoming a new little brother or sister to our family. They were aged eight and eleven at this time. We decided that at the next scan, the twenty-week scan, we would find out the gender of our new baby Gilson, we would also take the girls with us to the appointment. They were just as excited as us to find out whether we were to welcome a boy or a girl! Finding out the gender hadn't been an option for me when I was pregnant with the girls, so it was something entirely new and we were all very excited. I had an overwhelming feeling that it was a boy.

I was visiting an obstetrician privately and, on the 2nd of July 2002, off we set, full of excitement and anticipation. Oddly, I hadn't been feeling well and had become irritable but thought it was just hormones and put it down to the fact that I was always tired. I knew from the moment the scan started that there was a problem. It didn't look right, and they were checking my dates and asking too many questions.

"Is everything okay?" I asked, *"Can you see whether it's a girl or a boy?"* clinging to the tiniest hope that all would be well.

There were two people in the room apart from us, it was a new ultrasound scanner and the staff were being trained on it, as I recall. Strange the things you remember. *"Are you absolutely certain of your dates?"* I was asked. *"There seems to be a problem, you'll have to speak to the doctor!"*

I sat back in the waiting room with my concerned little family around me. *"It must be because of the new scanner"* I thought, but deep down I was beginning to feel very uneasy. The girls sensed that something was wrong but none of us could vocalise it or wanted to in a waiting room full of people. When my name was called, we all trooped into the obstetrician's office together.

"I'm so sorry," she said, *"but the baby has stopped growing. There isn't enough amniotic fluid. It appears he stopped growing at around eighteen weeks."*

At this point Steve then took the girls back into the waiting room. *"Isn't there anything you can do?"* I asked her in desperation; she shook her head. *"Is it possible that things could change and that this could turn around somehow?"* I was desperately clutching at straws.

"Not in my experience" she replied, holding my gaze. *"Go home and wait for nature to take its course. Make an appointment for two weeks' time and, if you need anything before that or anything happens in the meantime, just call me."*

"What if anything happens in the night?" I asked her.

"Have a bag packed and call me straight away," she replied.

I found her cold and matter of fact attitude incredibly painful. There was no empathy whatsoever and also very little in the way of explanation, I was completely stunned. So much so that, when I returned home, I had to phone her for clarification. I left the clinic in complete and utter shock and despair. The journey home was silent. My youngest tried to make us smile, as she always did, but Steve, uncharacteristically, told her to *"Shut up!"* He was struggling too, not knowing how to cope with all the emotions he suddenly found swirling around his head. He didn't know how he would be able to make this better for us all. But of course, he just couldn't, no one could; it was impossible. His main concern then was how he was going to help us all, especially me as he knew how much it meant to me, plus he was trying to wrap his head around what would happen next. I couldn't reassure anyone either as I was completely floored and honestly didn't understand or know what was happening myself, or what would actually happen next. However, I would soon find out.

I had, as previously stated, mistakenly thought that once you passed the twelve weeks stage that nothing could go wrong, unless at the actual delivery itself. You don't really know these things until it happens to you or someone close to you. Once back home, I tried to make everything as normal as possible for the girls, but thoughts were whirling around in my head.

"Was it something I had done?"

Why? Why was this happening to me? Had I been too greedy, had I wanted too much?"

On and on the thoughts continued. I hardly slept that night. I was completely heartbroken, cradling my pregnant belly while tears rolled down my cheeks and plopped onto the pillow. I phoned one of my close friends, Helen, who is a midwife. Helen works at the main hospital in Malta and as a midwife could help to explain what was actually going on. The first thing was that she didn't think I should wait two weeks, for my mental health as much as my physical, and also possible concerns about blood poisoning, so she arranged for me to go to hospital and see a consultant a few days later. Helen told me to prepare a bag, as I may need to stay in. I spoke to the girls as gently as I could and they went to stay at their grandparents for the day, and possibly the night, I can't remember. I expect so though as Steve stayed with me all night.

I met Helen at the hospital and, after speaking to the consultant, we went for an ultrasound. I remember lying there and the midwife looked sad, *"I'm sorry,"* she said, *"I can't find a heartbeat."* Although I had been expecting this news, I still felt sick. I wondered when his heart had stopped. The tears then started to flow; I don't remember when they eventually stopped. We went back to the consultant's office, and I recall one pregnant woman complaining that I was jumping the queue. We said nothing, but all the time I wanted to scream at everyone in that waiting room who were casting evil glances my way, *"My baby is dead! Is that a good enough reason for you!"*

The consultant, an obstetrician, said I could go home if I wanted to prepare myself, or I could stay in now if I was ready. I told him that I had a bag and was ready as Helen had already prepared me and explained that this might happen. What I actually wanted was for him to say, *"You can stay in hospital, and we will bring the baby back to life. All will be well; we just have to monitor you."* That was my dream version at least. I thought that if I had been much further along in the pregnancy when the problem was discovered, when there was still a heartbeat, that things may have been different, of course no one knows that as there are too many scenarios of possible outcomes. Instead, we headed up to the ward, where I met one of the most compassionate people I have ever met in my life, the head of the ward, Marcelle. Then, while she explained what would happen next, Steve finally broke down and she comforted him, whilst Helen continued to comfort me. None of this was easy; it was the worst day of my life. It was the 6th of July 2002.

I was admitted and went to a single room. Thankfully, Steve was allowed to stay with me. I think he went home just to let the girls know what was happening but then returned with a few things that we had been told we might need - a camera, a soft toy and a blanket, things that I hadn't thought to pack. Well, you don't, do you? Those midwives, and especially Helen, will have my undying gratitude for eternity, their empathy and gentleness went above and beyond.

I had to go through the physical and mental pain of labour and delivery, but it wasn't anywhere near the pain I felt in my heart. I felt as though someone had stuck a knife into the centre of my heart and it had shattered into a million pieces. The staff were wonderful. My dear friend Helen stayed with me, apart from popping home to see her own family briefly and then returning.

Helen was with me, along with the midwife who had delivered both of my girls, when Ian came into the world sleeping. He was perfectly formed just tiny, like a little doll, I could already tell that he was the image of his dad. We held him and spoke to him tenderly; we kissed him goodnight on his little head. We also took a few photographs as that would be all we had in the end, although the memory is forever etched into my heart and mind. I didn't want to give him back to the midwife, but sadly I had to, he was incredibly fragile. We had decided that no one else would see our little boy, just us, I felt that it might have been too much for the girls to endure, too traumatic for them. Was that the right thing to do? I don't really know but I just went with what I felt was the right thing to do at the time. We were given a little white pouch which contained his hand and footprints and his hospital bracelet. Tests would be made to try and ascertain what had happened. Nothing was conclusive, but the lack of amniotic fluid, oligohydramnios, could have been an indicator that his kidneys weren't functioning, however no-one knew for sure.

Steve slept by my side that night as I flitted in and out of sleep. I would remind Steve at times of the people we had to contact: my family and friends abroad, all who had known about our pregnancy, none of whom knew that things had taken a dire turn. This was possibly the hardest job and poor Steve had to find the courage to do this on his own; he is incredibly strong. The next day, Steve brought the girls in to see me. It was a Sunday, so they were allowed to visit. They hugged me tightly and I tried to put on a brave face for them. As I brushed the little one's hair, I thought *'I will never get to brush my little boy's hair'* I was holding back the tears as my throat constricted with all the unshed pain; I couldn't imagine where so many tears came from, I felt if I started again I would never stop, and I wanted to protect the girls and to make them think that I was fine but they knew that I wasn't of course. That whole first year was littered with those kinds of thoughts. I told the girls how wonderful the staff and people at the hospital had been, and this contributed to my oldest daughter becoming a midwife herself. This is something I am enormously proud of. She is exactly the right character for this job - compassionate and caring but also strong and practical in equal measures. The arrival of our son under such sad circumstances did bring Steve and I closer together as we bonded in our grief.

Steve and the girls got me through it; we got each other through it as a family. I had to carry on with some kind of routine and I felt truly blessed that I had my girls, I don't know how I would have got through it without them. They were and still are my world. My youngest was such an entertainer and constantly tried to cheer me up, succeeding much of the time. My oldest was a quiet, comforting presence. I received a lot of love and support from friends and family near and far, and in particular from my group of girlfriends, *'The Foreign Wives Club'*. These are foreign women who were married to Maltese men and with whom we formed our own little club/support group in lieu of our own families. They really helped and supported all of us. Steve's family decided that it was best not to talk about it and never contacted me or spoke to me about it again; a fact that I struggled with at the time, I now understand that everyone has their own ways of dealing with things and that is something I just have to accept. Maybe they just didn't have the capacity for it. I tried so hard to make life normal for the girls, although now I don't think I really managed to achieve that, unfortunately.

Steve and I went to a support group that was enormously helpful for me. I'm not sure it was for Steve, but he attended anyway to support me. His way of dealing with grief, and things in general, is to throw himself into work, keep busy and not talk about it. Doing that means it somehow goes away for him. Personally, I don't think that's at all healthy, but each to their own and I have learnt that we all have our own way of dealing with things, especially grief; it is so very individual. I expect it was due to the way he was brought up, since his family acted in the exact same way. We met other grieving parents, and we supported and comforted each other. Steve and I were the only ones in the group that already had children - as I said, an absolute blessing, although I know that others in the group did go on to have their own families. We decided to try again for another baby, I mistakenly thought that it would help to heal the pain, especially as my longing for another child had not gone away. In reality, it helped me to accept the situation, but sadly I had to eventually admit that it wasn't meant for us. We were so blessed to have our girls and we loved them so much. That fact certainly played a huge part in my recovery.

Life continued and time, although it doesn't actually heal the grief you feel, does help you to learn to live with it. It is something that you just learn, you carry it with you. I held Ian for the first and last time in July and slowly I started to recover and heal, albeit very slowly.

Tapestry made for me by my friend and midwife Helen.

14th July 2002

My darling Ian,

I want to start this book for you because, as time passes, I want to remember everything, as painful as that might be. I also need somewhere to pour all the love I have for you. All my thoughts and feelings for you. Not because I will ever forget you, but with time, memories of feelings fade. I love you so much that sometimes I feel my heart will break. I will always love you and you will forever have a special place in my heart. You became a part of me the second that I knew you existed. From the very first moment that I discovered that I was pregnant, my love for you began and it grew deeper and deeper with every passing day. You were my baby and I loved you. You were and always will be a part of me.

When you arrived too early, I thought that my heart would break. I held you in my arms, stroked your face and head. Kissed you and talked to you. I told you that I would always love you but couldn't keep you. I had to give you back, you were asleep my darling baby boy. Gone from me for now, but I am certain that we will meet again. I pray you are being kept safe for me until then, but I can't help wondering about what would have been, how much you would have enriched our lives, as I'm certain you would.

You were just so perfect, tiny little hands and feet. You have feet just like daddy, long and slim, even your legs were just like that too. I think you would have been like him, in appearance anyway. I will always wonder what your character would have been like. Your sisters are so different. I also wonder what colour your eyes would have been.

I was so unbearably sad to lose you, to have to let you go. When I discovered I was pregnant with you, I cried with joy! You were my dream come true! Everything was going so well, and we went on holiday to England. I couldn't resist buying you a few things. I haven't been able to pack them away yet, one was a little white snowsuit since you would be a winter baby. At the nine weeks scan, you measured ten weeks; I had a feeling you were a boy at this point. At thirteen weeks, I saw you again and your little heart was beating, you looked so sweet. Then, at seventeen weeks, I was told you had a strong heartbeat, I was so hopeful that all would be well with you. We had started talking to you, I wonder did you hear us?

Everything started to go terribly wrong for us at twenty weeks, the ultrasound showed that you had stopped growing at eighteen weeks and that you weren't moving, but your heart was still beating. I knew something was very wrong. I was told that there wasn't much amniotic fluid.

My saddest thought was that you were in pain, I know that not having enough fluid makes it painful for you to move. I am so sorry if that was the case for you; I didn't realise. I was told to wait but my fears for you made me seek advice from my friend Helen. I hoped against all odds that you would be okay, and everything would be alright. However, sadly this was not the case.

When I went to hospital and found that your heart had stopped beating, that you had died, I thought my own heart had stopped but my heart had just started to break. After labour was induced, daddy and I waited for your arrival. I was so sad but in a way longing to see you. I now knew and accepted the fact that it was inevitable, the pain, however, was unbearable. The pain of knowing that I couldn't keep you, not the labour pain. You arrived at 7.20pm, my darling baby boy, our son. We named you Ian Stephen. Ian was the name that daddy always wanted for his son and Stephen was of course after daddy. We kept you for just half an hour. Daddy held you too and then we kissed you goodbye. We took some photographs and your footprints and handprints. These are my precious memories, together with your identification bracelet. I haven't got the photo's yet, but I hope to have them soon - although your image is etched into my memory forever. The worst thing of all was leaving the hospital without you, my arms empty, having to leave you behind, my precious baby boy. It's an emptiness and ache that defies explanation.

You have two sisters; they were also very upset to lose you. They sent a teddy bear to hospital for you. Rebecca is the oldest, and she is thoughtful, kind and considerate. She was so looking forward to having a baby at home and would have been very hands on with your care I'm sure. Then there is Sarah, who is the life and soul of everything. She is a bubbly little character who was also looking forward to being a big sister and having a baby at home, she would have loved playing with you. Your dad is a very good man, hardworking, loving and cares so much for his family. We cried together endlessly for our great loss, for you.

It was the worst experience of my life and I so wish it could have been different. I keep wishing that you were still safely growing inside me. I wake up still thinking you are there and then the reality hits all over again. I am trying to be strong for daddy, Becky and Sarah and the other people around me, but inside I am crying and silently screaming 'I just want my baby back.' Daddy is trying to help me by taking me out, I don't feel like it but I'm trying. As much as I hate to admit it, life must go on. I ache with longing to hold, feed and nurture you; it is literally a physical pain. Whatever happens and even if we have another baby in the future, they will never be able to replace you.

Many people phoned, called round, sent flowers and cards; they were all very kind. There's really nothing that anyone can do because nothing can bring you back. Daddy and I are going to a support group, where other people have had similar losses. It is so sad, but eventually it may help us both and bring us some acceptance. Your loss has brought daddy and I closer together and I want to hold onto that.

In a few weeks we will have the results of the tests and maybe some answers. It won't change anything, but it might help us to understand what happened. November will be a difficult time as that is your original due date, and it will now be when we have your funeral.

That's all I can say for now my darling boy. Please know that I love you with all my heart and always will.

Forever and always,

Mummy xxxxxx

Dealing with Loss and Grief: How to Help

It is so important to remember to be mindful in the face of someone's loss. Here are some important things to remember: -

Things not to say to someone who has recently had a miscarriage or lost a baby in pregnancy.

"Be grateful, at least you already have a child/children."

"Be grateful for what you have."

"It wasn't meant to be."

"Miscarriage is more common than you think and happens to a lot of people."

"Well, at least you know you can get pregnant."

"Maybe you should have/shouldn't have…"

"You can try again."

"I understand how you feel."

"Why would you want that at your age?"

"Everything happens for a reason."

"At least it was early."

And more in the same vein.

- Don't say, *"At least . . ."* …

- Don't say, *"You can try again soon"* …

- Don't say, *"I'm sure . . ."* ...

- Don't say, *"This is really common, more common than you think"* ...

- Don't say anything that projects your belief system onto someone else …

Grief is a very important emotion and needs to be felt and worked through. Grief is also individual - everyone deals with it differently and in their own way. It's not a question of being ungrateful; we are grieving the loss of a baby and all that that entails, the future of our child, and also a sibling for our other child/children.

'It's just one of those things' was another one, it might be to you, but it certainly isn't to the parents/siblings of that baby.

Whilst well meaning, believe me, it really isn't helpful and can in fact be very upsetting. Some of the above were said to me and, whilst I understand most of it was well meaning, it didn't help - on the contrary it was extremely hurtful. I was actually told at my six-week post-delivery follow-up, *"Well it's better than having a disabled child."* Can you imagine!

I was shocked and found this extremely distressing and actually replied, *"I would give anything to have him back here with me, no matter what was wrong."*

This did then get a response of *"Well, yes, I do understand, but you don't know what the future holds."* Whilst I wouldn't have wanted him to suffer in any way, we didn't actually know what was wrong or what caused him to stop growing, and initially I would have given anything to have him back no matter what.

I received flowers and cards from friends and family and all of them brought me some comfort in the fact that I knew that they were all thinking of me and that I was cared for.

Think before you speak. Be sensitive. If you know someone going through this or a similar situation, just be there for them, offer comfort and support.

A hug, a shoulder to cry on, lend a helping hand. I think some of the best things to say, if you're going to say anything, are: -

"I love you,"

"I'm sorry,"

"I'm here for you,"

"This is not your fault,"

"What can I do to help?"

Bear in mind that this may not be their first loss – approximately one in five pregnancies end in miscarriage. Please above all else, be kind. A few people had pointed out to me that maybe I was stupid to consider a child after the age of 40, with all the complications that can bring. Not helpful!

6th August 2002

My darling Ian,

One month has already passed since I held you. Time moves on and I still ache with the longing to hold you; my heart still hurts. I haven't been well over the last few weeks, but it's going to take time. I wish with all my heart that you were still growing inside me, but sadly wishing that won't make it so. I would give anything to have you back! The other day I fell asleep on the sofa - I haven't been sleeping well you see. Whilst I was sleeping, I felt that you were in my arms, warm and soft. I was cradling you next to me and it was so real. I woke up crying as it was just so palpable and I almost felt that you would still be there, of course you weren't, and it was a sad reminder that you had gone.

Your sister Sarah had her birthday yesterday, she was nine. I tried to make it the best I could for her and not allow my own sorrow to affect the day. We had a bowling party and a Harry Potter cake, that's her favourite at the moment. I felt sad thinking that you would never hug her and get to show your love for her as we do, but also that you won't be here to celebrate birthdays with us, and that equally we wouldn't get to celebrate any of your birthdays with you.

We won't watch you grow into a young man and celebrate each milestone on the way. Your first birthday, Christmases, your first day of school, the list goes on and on…

Next week we are going on holiday. You were supposed to be coming with us, safely cossetted in my womb, but that has all changed now. I feel so sad to have had to leave you behind, but it will be good for us all to reconnect as a family. We are going to Austria and Switzerland so that will be nice, we will escape from the heat. It's very hot here at the moment.

Daddy and I are still going to the support group. This week we have a doctor talking to us, but it makes no difference really; the doctor can't bring you back to me and we don't have the test results yet. I passionately believe that no matter who you are, unless you have been through this situation, you can't fully understand how we feel and the pain we are still suffering. The meetings bring some comfort in that we are acknowledging your very existence, my darling boy.

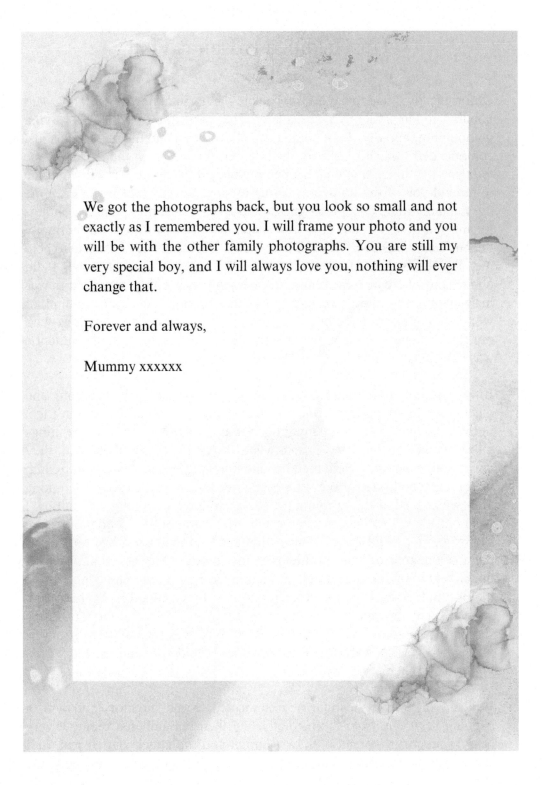

We got the photographs back, but you look so small and not exactly as I remembered you. I will frame your photo and you will be with the other family photographs. You are still my very special boy, and I will always love you, nothing will ever change that.

Forever and always,

Mummy xxxxxx

Unscheduled Hospital Visit

Unfortunately, I had to have a trip back to the hospital not long after we said goodbye to Ian, about two weeks later. The worst thing for me was leaving without him, but after I got home my milk came in and the pain of this just compounded the pain I already had, it felt like a slap in the face. No one tells you the things that then happen to your body and how it will continue to remind you of the trauma of losing a baby. So, in an effort to keep me busy and my mind occupied I guess, Steve was constantly planning outings for me and things to do. This was uncharacteristic of Steve, I'm normally the one who plans everything, but he meant well and was just trying to help me, I realised that. However, it was all a bit too much for me. I did understand where he was coming from though, as keeping busy for him was his way of dealing with everything, like that he didn't have time to think or wonder what might have been. I just wanted to wallow and be alone with my grief. We both thought that how the other was dealing with the situation was unhealthy.

It was a Friday night, and we went out with our friends, Rita and Paul, and our four children, partly to celebrate our wedding anniversary, I didn't feel in the least like celebrating anything, but again in an effort to make things more normal for everyone off we went, the children would enjoy it, they always did when they were together and knowing that gave me the strength to get ready and go out. We were going out for a meal. However, not long after we arrived at the restaurant, I started to have breathing difficulties. I went outside with Rita to try and catch my breath, but I just couldn't seem to breathe; I was gasping for air. I thought I was having a heart attack as there is a history of heart problems in my family. Our friends kindly took the girls home with them and kept them overnight, while Steve took me to the hospital. A lot of tests were carried out, ECG, blood tests and so on, after this they decided to keep me in as my heart rate was erratic, and they started me on some preventative medication. I was beginning to hate this place and I was so scared - scared now that I would die and leave my girls without a mother.

Whilst lying in my hospital bed connected to the monitors and with a banging headache from the medication, I then remembered seeing a very heavily pregnant woman at the restaurant and the attack started just after she arrived. It was not her fault, of course, but it triggered something in me and, contrary to what I initially thought, I actually believe it was an anxiety attack, it was all the same symptoms. Tests continued and I was booked in to have an angiogram. After a week, I went home. I had missed the girls so much, I wished I could have spared them this extra pain; one trauma was surely enough. However, it seems it never rains but it pours, but that's how things go in life after all. Tests were inconclusive and life carried on, albeit without my darling boy.

6th September 2002

My darling Ian,

It's been two months and I still can't believe it. I keep imagining how many weeks pregnant I should have been now. If only you could have stayed just a bit longer maybe, they would have been able to save you, I know I'm just clutching at straws and I know that things may not have been perfect with you, but I would still prefer that you were here - although I want you to know that I wouldn't want you to ever suffer in anyway whatsoever.

We had a nice holiday; it was nice to get away, but my thoughts were with you a lot of the time. However, I tried to make it special for your sisters, for they have been suffering too. We stayed in a lovely place. We went up a mountain called Mount Titlis on a cable car. There was a lot of snow, and the girls built a snowman, they had so much fun. We also went to Gardaland and on a boat on Lake Lugano. I lit candles for you at all the churches we went to visit, and I prayed that you are now in a better place.

My feelings of grief and loss just wash over me without any warning, and I find myself crying, although I am beginning to come to terms with what has happened. It's beginning to dull just a little, like a numbness almost.

We have a new kitten too. Sarah found him and we've called him Tiger. Initially there were two kittens but only this one stayed. He is lovely and dad has let him stay. Your sisters have wanted another kitten for a long time, so here he is!

We've had most of the test results back now, but there were no answers. They found nothing wrong with you or me, just one of those things. I hate that expression; how can that be? I really thought we'd have answers - an explanation which might have helped us to accept it in some way. The support group has also now finished, and I cried at the last session but now it's over. One of the couples are expecting another baby, I hope all goes well for them this time.

Your sister wrote some poems for you, and they break my heart too. It has affected both of your sisters so profoundly and I wish above all else I could take away their pain. Rebecca will be twelve next week and I want her to have a special day; she is going to swim with dolphins. I am so desperately trying to give them some happy memories this year too, but as always, I will also be thinking of you. I would be 7 months pregnant now and I think of you every day. Last week I held some of the baby clothes I had bought for you and wept because holding them without you in them was so incredibly painful. I haven't been able to put them away yet, it's just a matter of time.

I love you Ian,

Forever and always,

Mummy xxxxxx

My little baby

I am young but still I have a child in heaven,
and nothing is harming our love so strong
our love so strong and true,
I would climb mountains high for his that will
not die, for I fear my love is high.

A baby called Ian

A little baby so sweet and small
I even wish I could take him to the Mall,
I am young I am not even fifty-seven
I wish I wish I could go up to heaven
Just to see a little baby boy so-
sweet & charming that I had to call him Ian

12th November 2002

My darling Ian,

Today is my due date; the end of the forty weeks. I doubt you would have arrived exactly on this date, since your sisters didn't arrive on their due date. I know that it is highly unlikely, but somehow it marks another milestone.

All the results are back now, and they are all negative, so we still have no answers. I often wonder what could have happened and if it was something I did, or maybe it was your kidneys, I looked up Oligohydramnios, which is a deficiency of amniotic fluid and causes problems during pregnancy, but we will never know for sure.

This month the pain is so acute again as I keep thinking that by now you would have been with us, and that life would have been so hugely different. I really miss you. I know that sounds strange as you were never really here, but I knew you; I nurtured you inside me. I know what it's like to have a newborn baby, to hold and cherish them, watching them grow. Such a wonderful feeling!

I miss all that and more, again wondering what kind of person you would have been. This month is also my birthday, but it just won't be the same this year. Daddy is buying me a locket to put your photo in and then you will always be near me, and I can keep you close to my heart.

The funeral has been arranged for the 27th of November, and you will be laid to rest at last. I'm sure it will be an incredibly sad day, but I have to say my farewell to you. Your sisters are coming too. Sarah keeps a photo of you in a little heart she has, and I am keeping Becky's photo for her for now. I have a photo of you in the sitting room with the other family photos, because more than anything I want to acknowledge you as part of our family; to include you. I am also going to have a star named after you. It's in your memory and also your Christmas present. There is so little I can do for you now, but this is something nice, something to mark your existence, which will last forever

It will soon be Christmas, my favourite time of year, but it will be tough this year. I will be thinking of you and remembering that my love for you is constant and will always be there; it will never ever diminish.

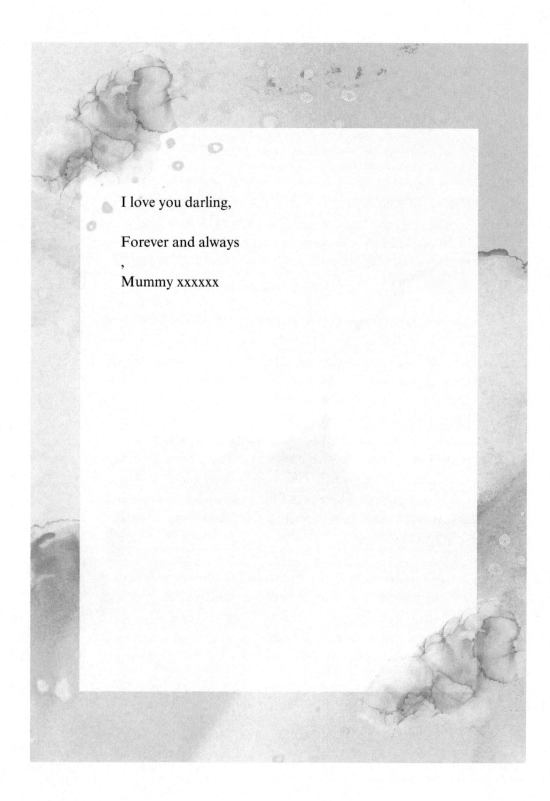

I love you darling,

Forever and always
,
Mummy xxxxxx

The Funeral – 27th November 2002

A communal burial was arranged for November at the end of the year. November in Malta is the month that we remember the dead. I'm not sure if this is the reason that it takes place in November or not, but it seemed to make sense.

Apparently, this takes place every year - a fact I wish I didn't know. The communal burial is for all babies born under a certain weight and gestation. Again, I had no idea of what would happen. I had thought we would plan our own funeral, but apparently to be viable the baby has to be over a certain age or time frame, I believe that is 24 weeks, although that could have changed. In a way, it was one less heart-breaking thing for us to have to consider or plan. So, just as I was beginning to heal, it was like the plaster being ripped off all over again. I asked the girls if they would like to attend the funeral, for I felt they were old enough to make that decision for themselves. They decided to come. It gave them a chance to say goodbye to their brother and I hoped also to find some closure, for all of us.

Steve carried the coffin into the church; he was just in the right place at the right time. We arrived at the same time as the coffin - it wasn't planned like that. The coffin was so very small. It was white and painted with water lilies. I remember thinking how pretty it was. A lot of effort had gone into the day, and I really did appreciate that. The service went well, or as well as could be expected. There were people from the support group there too, so there were people there that we knew, this helped somewhat. I went to light a candle at the altar. I believe I was shaking but we all did it, each couple, and that also made it a little easier - it is why I always light a candle for Ian whenever I am in a church now. We all had a flower to throw onto the coffin after it had been lowered into the ground. I had also given Marcelle a teeny tiny teddy to be buried with Ian. I kissed it for him, it was all I could do. I also keep the same teddy here with me. I had ordered flowers for the day: a white cushion with white miniature roses and blue ribbon from Steve and I and a heart also with white miniature roses and blue ribbon from the girls. Friends had asked if they should come, I told them there was no need.

Shortly afterwards, I returned to work; the following month, I think. That also helped me to resume the routine that I had had before. The love and support I received from my boss and his family was invaluable. I will be forever grateful for their love and kindness at what was such a very difficult time for me.

24th December 2002

My darling Ian,

It's been a while since I last wrote, but it's Christmas Eve and I have been thinking about you so much over the last few days. I would give absolutely anything to have you here with us to celebrate, even the sleepless nights.

Whilst wrapping presents, I've thought of the things we would have bought for you - baby's first Christmas outfits and trinkets, although you would have been too young to really know. We will be lighting a candle for you tomorrow; something so small but hugely significant for us. A Christmas Memorial Mass was held and families suffering the loss of a baby, at whatever stage, came together. It was a form of support, some of the families had been grieving for a long time, but I don't think we will go again. It's not something I feel I need to do to remember you.

So, I go through the motions, the presents have been bought and wrapped and the cards written – I actually wrote a card with your name on it, just to see how it would feel, I kept the card with your other memories.

'*Merry Christmas, with love from Janet, Steve, Becky, Sarah & Ian*'

Yesterday Becky and Sarah came with me to the cemetery to leave you some flowers. We left a poinsettia plant for Christmas; it's all that we can do now. The pain now is as bad as when we lost you, and honestly, I'm finding it hard to cope, whilst trying to keep going and not to show the rest of the family or let it affect them. The girls seem to sense it though and are extremely caring and supportive. Tomorrow I will try hard to make it as special as I can for them, but you will be constantly in my thoughts.

The burial last month was very painful. When I had to go and light a candle for you and place it on the altar, I thought my heart had shattered into a million pieces again.

It was just so hard to say goodbye all over again. We all cried, and daddy helped to carry the coffin. It was painted with beautiful water lilies. I kept thinking we should be lighting this candle for your baptism and not for your funeral.

I keep your photo in my locket and wear it most of the time. I miss you so much. I wouldn't have thought it possible to miss someone so much when that someone wasn't really with you for long.

You now have a star in the heavens with your name on it.

Happy Christmas my darling, I love you so much.

Forever and always,

Mummy xxxxxx

Universal Star Listing

This certifies that the Universal Star Listing hereby designates the star having the co-ordinates:

Cygnus   20h06m17s +31°47'55"

the following name:

Ian Stephen Gilson

This name is permanently recorded in our listing, which will be published and copyrighted in our book to be deposited with the British Library.

I bear witness to this registration, with the official seal of the Universal Star Listing, as recorded on:

12 November

2002

Registrar

27th February 2003

My darling Ian,

A New Year has begun, and I look forward with some optimism to the future, whether that holds a new baby for us or not. Of course, a new baby could never replace you but I'm hoping it will at least go some way to healing my heart a tiny bit. I am getting on with daily life again, going through the motions. I still often find myself thinking about how different life would be now if you were here with us, when I'm walking, I imagine pushing a pram.

I do now feel a strange sort of letting go. Not that that means I've left you behind, far from it, you are always in my thoughts and your picture is always with me. I do still have moments when I wish you were here with us, but I've reached a state of acceptance now, knowing that this is how it has to be.

A strange thing happened when I dropped your frame and broke your angel (which Daddy has now fixed, now you know why we call him Mr. Fix It!) I felt that I hadn't let you go and that by doing that I might be preventing your spirit from moving on. I really wouldn't want that. I want you to be loved and happy wherever you are. In my search for answers and healing I was reading a book about a woman who died and came back to life again (how I wish that was you). She describes a feeling of overwhelming love, like nothing she's ever felt before. I wish with all my heart that that is the feeling you have. I can't imagine anyone loving you more than me, but I do accept it could be possible.

In this quest I also turned to the church, but they didn't have answers either other than it's just one of those things - not that easy to accept, unfortunately.

Next week I am going away. I am going to see your nanny and grandad in England; they would have loved you so very much too. Daddy, Becky and Sarah are staying here in Malta, so that should be interesting.

It is the first time that I will be leaving all three of them alone together without me. I can't imagine them coping very well, but I guess they will have to. I'm sure they'll muddle through somehow; I just need a short break away from everything.

I love and miss you with all my heart.

Forever and always,

Mummy xxxxxx

Having a Baby After 40

Although I realised that having a baby after forty may have more complications, I assumed that this was merely for first time mums, so it didn't actually apply to me, I was wrong! However, I had heard about many women having a successful pregnancy at that age. I was bolstered by famous women, like Madonna, Jane Seymour, etc., they filled me with false hope, (remember this was 2002) I ended up thinking, *"Why them and not me?"* I hadn't expected it to be so difficult. Unlike the rich and famous, for the majority of women it is not that simple.

However, fast forward twenty-one years, and, due to advances in technology surrounding fertility, pregnancy, and delivery, we are told that it's completely possible to safely have a baby at age forty. In fact, it is becoming increasingly more common. Rates of first-time mums between the ages of 40-44 have risen considerably; they have actually more than doubled in the last twenty years. Many young women are also opting to freeze their eggs for use at a later date, which is an option, for varying reasons. This is understandable, if a little expensive. Be that as it may, any pregnancy after the age of forty is still considered 'high risk', both for the health of the mother and the baby. Midwives and obstetricians will monitor the pregnancy closely. Whilst the pregnancy itself can also be more challenging, it can still be achieved, often with a little help. It is though also advisable to see a fertility specialist for tests.

The CDC advises that thirty percent of woman ages 40 to 44 will experience infertility. Chances of conceiving in any given month are also lower once you pass the big 4-0! A forty-year-old only has a five percent chance of getting pregnant per month. This is also confirmed by the Office on Women's Health, which states that one third of couples after the age of 35 experience fertility issues. This may be attributed in part to the following risk factors: fewer number of eggs, unhealthy eggs, ovaries unable to release eggs properly, increased risk of miscarriage and higher chances of health conditions that can impact fertility.

This means that, even for those that will get pregnant, it may take longer. Of course, there are a lot more fertility options now too, including IVF, egg freezing, sperm banks and surrogacy (in some countries). While women are often told it's best to have children before the age of thirty-five, the new data may possibly suggest otherwise.

Even with all these options available, it needs to be noted that a woman's fertility rate does decrease significantly after thirty-five years of age.

There are undeniably some benefits to having a baby later in life, and it is also down to individual choice. Of course, there are of course obvious challenges, but the benefits include being better emotionally prepared and ready to focus more on family life. The prospective parents are also more likely to be more established in career paths and more settled financially. Children can be very expensive and that might be a factor; it is less overwhelming at a later stage in your life. You may also have ticked a lot of things off your bucket list, including such things as travelling. On the other side of the coin is whether you will have the energy. Obviously, this is all then down to the individuals and their lifestyles.

Getting pregnant after forty is possible without fertility treatment, but your chances of having trouble conceiving are higher. After the age of forty-five, it's not likely that you'll be able to get pregnant with your own eggs, although there is always the exception, of course.

Having a baby at forty plus is more common than it used to be. Despite all the challenges along the way it is still a possibility, but you should really talk to a doctor about all the individual risk factors before starting down this route.

I visited a few obstetricians on my own journey. Sadly, they were not very helpful when I went to see them after I lost Ian. One told me that even if I could get pregnant, which was difficult in itself, then the chances of having a disabled child was very much higher, he spoke to me as if I was a child, using a milk bottle analogy! None of them were even remotely helpful or showed any empathy towards me at all. I found their attitudes very condescending; they only painted the negative side of things to me in an attempt to completely put me off trying again. However, as we now know, time of course, was not on my side.

MY STAR IN HEAVEN

I am sending
a dove to heaven
with a parcel on its wings
be careful when you open it
It's full of beautiful things
inside are a million kisses
wrapped up in a million hugs
to say how much I miss you
and to send you all my love.

I hold you close within my heart
and there you will remain
to walk with me
throughout my life
until we meet again.

- Author Unknown -

6th July 2003

My darling Ian,

This date is forever etched in my memory. I wonder if there will ever be a time where this day will pass and I won't remember how traumatic it was and how we had to say goodbye to you, together with our hopes and dreams for you. Life can be so cruel sometimes.

A year has passed already- how time flies! I can't believe how fast this last year has gone. Life has returned to a new normal, pretty much how it was before. I went back to work part-time, the girls continue at school, and we celebrate each new milestone in their lives. They keep me busy with various after school activities, Becky goes to ballet, which she loves and is very gifted at. Sarah continues to try new things all the time. I am not sure she will ever settle on just one thing in particular; she likes the diversity of many different outlets for her creative character. Currently that is learning to play the violin. She can turn her hand to most things when she puts her mind to it. I wonder what would have been your 'thing' and would you have shared any interests with them or with daddy or would you have tried out many new things before finding your passion?

I find that I am away from Malta at this time - was that deliberate I wonder? It certainly wasn't a conscious decision on my part, but maybe I needed to be away from the Island, to put some distance between the memory and the reality. I don't know really, but the thoughts and feelings are carried with me, just maybe it is a little easier like this.

I don't go to the cemetery as often anymore. Deep down I know that you are no longer there; your soul has moved on and is in a better place. I no longer need to be there to feel your presence and the love I have for you. It is a communal grave, maybe it would have been different if it was just yours, I don't really know, but I do know that I love you with all my heart and that will never ever change.

Forever and always

Mummy xxxxxx

The Angel of My Tears

How do you love a person
Who never got to be?
Or try to envision a face
You never got to see?
How do you mourn the death of one
Who never got to live?
When there's nothing to feel good about
And nothing to forgive?
I love you, my little baby,
My companion of the night.
Wandering through my lonely hours,
Beautiful and bright.
What does it mean to die before
You ever were born?
To live the lovely night of life
And never see the dawn?
Ah! My little baby,
You lived like anyone!
Life's a burst of joy and pain
And then, like yours, it's done.
I love you, my little baby,
Just as if you'd lived for years.
No more, no less, I think of you,
The angel of my tears.
~ Author Unknown

12th November 2003

My darling Ian,

This year we should be celebrating your first birthday and all your first milestones I expect you'd soon be walking, and I wish I could hold your little hand gently as you took those first tentative steps and hear your first words. "Mama" maybe? I still miss you so much. I think of you often and still wonder how our lives would have been if you had stayed with us.

At about this time, November, would have been your first birthday. We would have had such a big party for you my darling, just as we did for your sisters. First birthdays are such a momentous occasion here in Malta. We would have invited friends and family and had the Quccija. This is a tradition here in Malta wherein you choose something from a lineup of objects with varying meanings that is supposed to be an indication of what you would have chosen as a future career or how your life would have unfolded. I wonder what you would have chosen. Becky chose a book and Sarah chose money. It's all good fun and generally the highlight of the day.

What gifts would we have bought for you I wonder to myself? All kinds of things go through my mind, but it is useless. We always celebrate birthdays with a special day and party. I wonder if you would have liked that, your sisters certainly did! We had all sorts of parties for them: fancy dress, themes and parties at various locations. I imagine seeing your little face light up at the wonder of birthdays, balloons and parties. Presents and cards, just the general excitement of it all and another day for us all to join together as a family and just be together. I miss that so much.

Wherever you are, I am sending lots of love and so many hugs for your first birthday, my lovely precious boy.

Forever and always,

Mummy xxxxxx

The Quccija

Il-Quccija (the q is silent for non-Maltese speakers) is a fun Maltese tradition which is usually held at the baby's first birthday party. It dates back to the 18th century and is still very popular. It is a bit of party fun which is believed to predict the future career of the baby and/or their lifestyle.

Although many new updates have been added to it since then to reflect more modern times, there are still some of the traditional things left. These items are placed a few metres away from the baby and they crawl or walk towards the items, selecting which ever appeals to them the most. The first item chosen is said to be indicative of their future, it is both amusing and entertaining.

To give you some ideas, here are some examples of the items used and what they represent: -

- Stethoscope – Doctor

- Calculator – Accountant

- Paintbrush – Artist

- Computer mouse – IT

- Book – Author or journalist

- Credit Card – Banking

- Money – Professional businessperson

- Toothbrush – Dentist

- Hammer – A trade profession

- Hairbrush or comb – Hairdresser

- Rosary Beads or Bible – Nun or Priest

- Egg – A full and plentiful life

- Wooden spoon – Chef

- Make-up – Beauty industry

- The list goes on…

It is pretty obvious in most cases what the items represent and of course, you could add whatever you want really. It is the highlight of the first birthday party, and it is certainly charming. My eldest picked a book, whilst my youngest took the money after pondering the egg. Consumed with the excitement of it all, I let them choose another item!

9th March 2004

My darling Ian,

It has been a while since I last wrote, but it doesn't mean that I haven't been thinking of you because I have and, as you know, I speak to you too. I often think of things to write to you but somehow I never get round to putting pen to paper these days. There never seems to be enough time but, of course, it's all held within my heart and soul. Sometimes the grief is still so overwhelming, and I am caught by surprise at the depth of my feelings at these times. I should have written at Christmas, but I'm sure you feel the love I continue to send you.

I have been back to the cemetery, just once as I find the thought of going now so painful. Perhaps the thought is more painful than the actual act of doing so? I have left a small statue at the cemetery of a little boy with a ball. I also have one in the garden here at home so I can see it and think of you. It's my tribute to you and it replaces a headstone in my mind.

Sadly, at Christmas, our cat Tiger died after an illness. I had done everything I could for him, but he still died, poor little Tiger. Dad went out and brought back another cat called Sooty. He is very naughty and nearly knocked the Christmas tree over several times. I'm sure you would have loved him, just like the girls do. We've had so many pets in the last few years. Again, I wonder if you would have loved animals as much as your sisters. Sarah absolutely loves dogs and she spends a lot of time with the neighbors' dogs, but dad won't let her have one. He says we would end up looking after it, and he's probably right. So now we have Sooty. Our cats never seem to stay for very long, so we'll see.

Today I felt I had to write to you as I had a dream about you again last night. I like to detail the dreams just in case I forget, although that's unlikely, but then I will be able to look back at this and remember. I know it was you because it was so vivid, and I remember it so clearly. You were just so gorgeous, with brown hair and brown eyes. You were toddling about, but I held you in my arms and hugged you very tightly; it felt so good. You touched my cheek with your hand. You also said words from the nursery rhyme,

'Twinkle, Twinkle,
Little star,
Like a diamond in the sky.'

At first it didn't register, but then I realised that it all made sense. We had named a star after you, and your sister, Sarah, played it on her violin at a concert last Friday. I felt it was your way of letting me know that you are aware of what is going on within our family, your family. Maybe it was a visitation dream? It certainly left me with a warm glow. I have been asking and praying for a visit from you for so long, and now I feel that it has finally happened. There have been other baby dreams and I was never sure if it was you or not, but this time I was absolutely certain. It brought me so much joy.

To remind me of this day, I bought a 'Me to You' teddy bear which says 'A Hug from Me to You' on it, just for you. It really felt so special.

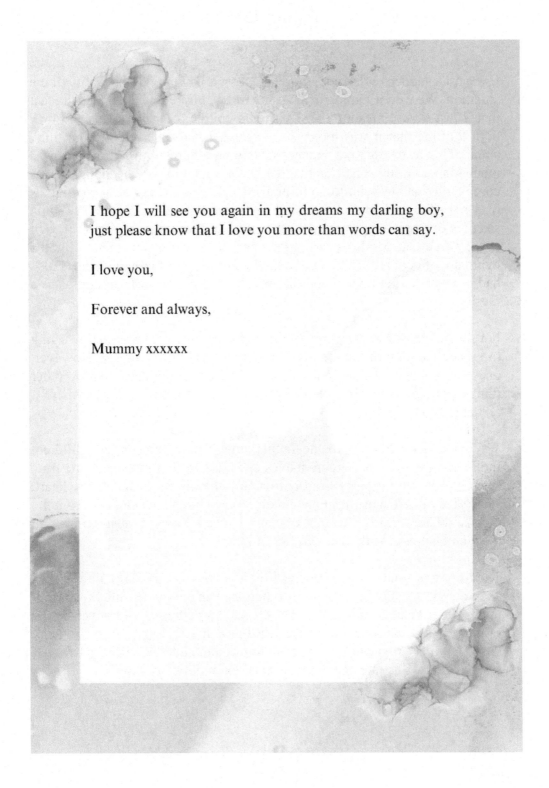

I hope I will see you again in my dreams my darling boy, just please know that I love you more than words can say.

I love you,

Forever and always,

Mummy xxxxxx

Acceptance

It wasn't a sudden realisation, more like a slow dawning of the reality of the situation. We weren't going to have any more children. I had to face the fact that it just wasn't meant to be. I visited a couple of obstetricians and they both told me that it was too risky, and that I had other children to think about. That at my age the chances of having a baby with a disability was much higher - things I had heard already. One actually said he thought I was completely mad to want to go through sleepless night and all the demands of a new baby. I didn't agree, and my other babies had been very good sleepers on the whole anyway. In the end however it was totally irrelevant as we weren't successful. I had another early miscarriage and then a blighted ovum so, of course for my own mental health, I eventually gave up. I also had to consider the impact that this was having on the girls and on us as a family.

For several years I was never in Malta on the 6th of July. I was clearly trying to escape the pain of the memory, although I didn't, obviously. However, once away from the Island, it was easier for me to be distracted by other things and put some distance between the pain of the memory of where it all happened.

We have new additions to the family now - new babies, new children. Indirectly, my dreams of more babies and a bigger family have come true. They are the tiniest part of me but occupy the biggest place in my heart. They give my life new meaning and direction at a time when I needed it the most and I am so fortunate to have them. I am overjoyed to spend time with them and help out with their care when I can.

They say that time is a healer, and it is in a way. As the days slowly pass and you put one foot in front of the other, carrying out your obligatory daily duties, your heart begins to piece itself back together. It will never be the same of course and the cracks are still there, but it slowly begins to heal. Although life will never ever be the same again, and you will never forget, one day you will smile again, and everything will be okay.

You Will be Okay

You will be okay,
No matter how intense the pain you currently feel.

You will be okay,
Time will eventually help to heal the wounds and put you
back together.

You will be okay,
Whatever the future has in store for you.

You will be okay,
Hold on my dear and just take one step at a time.

You will be okay,
The world will keep turning around you even though you
think it's stopped.

You will be okay,
Just believe that better days will come, they most
certainly will.

You will be okay,
You will smile again; you will laugh again one day.

You will be okay.

Janet Gilson 2023

6th July 2004

My darling Ian,

It is the second anniversary of when you were born sleeping, my darling, darling boy. I usually think of your birthday as November, when you were due. But today is also the day I remember you. Remembering holding you but then having to say goodbye to you, is still the hardest thing and it's just so sad. It will never be anything other than heart breaking.

Somehow life carries on without you, although sometimes I wonder how?! My heart still aches to hold you. My heart still breaks to feel your little hand in mine; for your hand to wrap itself around my finger; to watch all your milestones. I am so sad that I never got to look into your eyes and never got to hear your voice.

Healing and grieving are different for everyone, but for me it's been a long and difficult journey. The pain is unbearable at times. I veer between heartache and acceptance.

My throat seems to constrict so often with the pain of unshed tears, the tears I sometimes have to hold back. Occasionally the dam just bursts when I can no longer contain them, mostly when I am alone but occasionally when I talk about you to others. They say that when you can talk about something painful without crying then you know you have healed. I wonder if that will ever happen. I have heard that the grief never gets lighter, we just get used to carrying the weight, and this I do understand so well. Time marches on and in some ways, I feel you slipping from my grasp, but I find comfort in the fact that I firmly believe that we will be reunited again one day. The girls need me and so I have to show up for them and I do love them so much. I have to give them as normal a life as is possible, whatever normal is, but for me that has to be the life their friends enjoy, one without care at this age. I don't want them to carry my burdens. They are too young, and I want them to enjoy their childhood, as I would have wanted for you too. I never knew how many people had lost babies and had miscarriages; it's so much higher than I ever imagined.

I will spend this second anniversary thinking of you and imagining how you would look now. I think of your sisters at that age and a mixture of me and daddy, so I have an idea and from the pictures I have of you.

Rest well my baby boy.

I love you,

Forever and always,

Mummy xxxxxx

Foetomaternal Microchimerism

Foetomaternal microchimerism is something I've only just heard about. It is a phenomenon that occurs during pregnancy where foetal cells pass through the placenta and establish cell lineages within the mother. It involves bidirectional cross-placental trafficking during pregnancy, leading to a micro-chimeric state that can persist for decades. Sounds baffling, I know, but stick with me.

In various placental mammals, the bidirectional exchange of cells during pregnancy can lead to the acquisition of genetically unique cells that can persist in both mother and child for decades. Apparently, this is the case for however long you have been pregnant. Foetal cells cross the placenta and have been found in the mother even decades later. How cool is that?

Although the mother's immune system typically removes unchanged foetal cells from the blood after pregnancy, the ones that have already integrated with maternal tissues escape detection and therefore remain in the mother's body. Those foetal cells can be harboured in a mother's tissues where they become incorporated, lasting decades after the birth. This likely means that every mother's body contains both her own cells, genetics and tiny but measurable amounts of her children's cells and genomes.

And it gets even more beautiful: foetal cells have been observed to migrate to sites of injury in the mother's body, stimulating healing, and have even been found in caesarean scars. They've also been found to migrate to a mother's heart, potentially helping her to survive a heart attack.

It is comforting to know that a little part of those we love stays with us. I found this extremely comforting myself and thought that others might too, just knowing that a part of our babies remain with us; those that stayed with us and those that haven't.

24th December 2004

My darling Ian,

Another Christmas without you, but another ornament for you that hangs on the tree, and so we remember you in this way each year. There are a couple of Christmas stockings now hanging there just for you, my sweetheart.

You would now be two and so I think you would be getting excited for Christmas and the excitement of a visit from Father Christmas and the presents around the tree. There are lights on the tree outside the house for you - do you see them? We have decorated everywhere as we usually do, the tree is lit, and the presents wrapped.

I do love this time of year. I am all prepared for the girls to have a fabulous Christmas and to enjoy this time at home away from school with lots of family time together; apart from when your dad has to work, of course. I hope Sooty leaves the tree alone this year. Do you know he actually tries to climb it! He's a crazy cat!

We will light a candle for you, as always. You leave a little Ian-shaped hole in our family and our hearts, but we carry on without you.

Merry Christmas my darling boy.

Forever and always

Mummy xxxxxx

**The Memorial for Unborn Children by Martin Hudacek ©
2010**

21st September 2006

My darling Ian,

You are almost four. I love that age where we can talk and interact with each other, but you still have that air of being a baby around you. This month we had your sister Becky's sweet sixteen party. It was at the hotel where dad currently works. It was a lovely evening, although we didn't stay the whole night. Auntie Sheena and Uncle John happened to be here on holiday too, so that was nice. Becky has a boyfriend, has had for a couple of years now. His name is Colin, and he is very nice, quiet and shy. We have welcomed him into our family, his only fault is supporting Italy! Ha-ha!

I am all too aware that right now we would be preparing for your first day of school. I expect I would have kept you at home with me for as long as I could. I know how fast the time goes, having experienced this already with your sisters.

It's funny because your sister Becky has her school leaving right now; she will go on to college. She will have a Prom and get all dressed up in a long pink satin dress that we're having made for her. I have ordered a limo for her and her friends to take them to the Prom. It is all so much fun that again I wish you could be a part of, but I'm sure you're watching over us though.

I can't help but wonder where we would have chosen for you for school, since your sisters go to a girls' school. It wouldn't have been there, but it would have been nice to send you to somewhere that is similar, as it seems to suit your sisters very well. I wonder how you would have settled, whether you would have cried like Sarah, or just taken it in your stride, like Becky. I expect I would have cried, just as I did with your sisters. It's so hard that first day without them, but, of course, I have a lifetime without you.

In my mind, I can picture you in your little uniform. I long to hold you so tightly, to hug you close to me and whisper reassurances in your ears, then reluctantly let you go. I would have packed your lunch with such love and care and would worry about you all day. I would then be waiting for you when the day was over, waiting to welcome you back into the warmth and security of my arms, to somewhere that you are happy and familiar with. I would patiently wait to hear all about your day and hear your fun stories. You would also have had a first day gift from us, just as your sisters did, for this is something I liked to do. I'm sorry to keep comparing things to your sisters, but those are the experiences that I have, they are my benchmarks, and they come flooding back when I start to think about you and the stages we should be going through. It is a strange comfort in a way that I can compare and reflect on what your sisters did at the same age.

It's the little things that I wonder about - what would your favourite food be at the moment and what sandwiches would you take with you in your lunchbox?

I wonder what your little backpack would have on it. Currently, the popular things are Cars, Ice Age and the penguins from Happy Feet! I think it would be Cars, but I do love penguins. It's one of those things that I will always continue to wonder as time goes on.

I love you,

Forever and always,

Mummy xxxxxx

Attitude of Gratitude

Gratitude is a powerful and positive emotion that benefits our health and wellbeing. Why, you might ask, have I included this within a story that mainly deals with overcoming the grief of losing a baby? Well, for a glimmer of hope, a little optimism, and because I also want this book to be a book of hope. I have found that practicing gratitude is what works well for me. It has the ability to turn around my mood and thoughts. I don't think that negativity has a chance when you start to feel grateful for everything in your life. Whenever I feel negativity creeping in and think that I might start spiraling, I try to turn my thoughts around. It's not always easy, and, of course, I'm human, so there are days when I wallow, obviously. However, the important thing is not to pack up and live there.

Of course, it also depends where you are in your own grieving process, but this started quite early on in my journey. Of course, it is not for everyone, not straight away at least. My own mindset constantly tells me that there is always, always, someone worse off than me, then I count my blessings. I do use this a lot in my everyday life now anyway. Sometimes I wake up feeling a bit low so then I start counting my blessings.

It does take practice. Initially I used a gratitude journal; as a writer, I love to write! You can find many of these journals online, but you can use anything- a diary, a notepad or jotter. I still write them down at times, but often it's enough just to say them in my head as a reminder to myself, especially first thing in the morning when I'm barely awake, especially if I have woken with a black cloud above my head. The things that I am grateful for are often repetitive, and I find myself saying the same things, but that's fine too; it just serves as a reminder. I usually start when I wake up and am thankful for another day. Even if it is the dreariest day, I look for something to be grateful for and I try to add something into the day that would bring me some joy, no matter how small. If I find I don't have time in the morning, I will sometimes reflect on them in the evening before I sleep and then I think of the things that have given me cause to be grateful during that day, again it need only be something small.

Whilst realising that there are many people worse off than myself, obviously it doesn't in any way diminish my own loss at all. However, I feel it does help me gain some perspective and when I remember all the things that I have in my life, that makes me feel grateful for the life I have.

6th July 2009

My darling Ian,

So much time has passed since I last wrote. Life takes over and things are always so busy, but I still think of you often, you know that. Sometimes I just tell you things in my head and heart. I hope you still get the messages, wherever you may be. Then a special year arrives, and my mind automatically thinks of what we would or should have been doing, and how you should have been a part of it all.

This year you would have taken your first Holy Communion, so, of course, there would have been your catechism lessons leading up to that, and I can just imagine you all dressed up in your little suit just like a little young man; so many things that we miss out on. I am feeling a lot better though and I really hope that you are happy, wherever you are. I dreamt about you again. Whenever I dream about you, you are always playing with a ball and always in a white football strip - such a cutie. You always hug me and smile. You told me to look for signs; that they are all around.

The next day I found a little white feather, which I have kept. Thank you, my darling boy, for letting me know that your presence is always near me, I just need to recognize the signs.

Life has been busy. Your dad is still working nonstop and throws himself into anything; perhaps to dull the pain or just because that's how he is. In 2002, dad also bought a flat and he has developed it into a block, so that keeps him really busy. He is, and always will be, a workaholic.

Next month we have your sister Sarah's sweet sixteen. As you know we did one for Becky too, so we also have to do one for Sarah. It will be at the hotel where dad works again, but a different hotel now. I always like to make a fuss of their birthdays. Sarah also has her school leaving this year. She will go to college after this and she will also have a Prom, just like her sister, together with all her friends. Becky and Sarah both have very busy social lives now and usually have me or dad running them around.

We're like a taxi service, dropping them off at places and then picking them up when they are ready, but I prefer it that way at least I know they're safe. Dad says all he needs is a cap to be the chauffeur! I expect it would be the same with you and your life, certainly with the preparation for your first holy communion.

I miss you so much. I still have that little white snowsuit. I will never part with it. I can still hug it when I want to and think of you; it helps.

I love you,

Forever and always,

Mummy xxxxxx

***When feathers appear
A loved one is near!***

12th November 2012

My darling Ian,

This month you would have been ten - going into double figures! Time marches on and the years just roll on by, each one faster than the last. This month though we do have another celebration: we celebrate Becky's graduation as a midwife. She actually started working in August. This was an exciting time for us and one where we celebrated all Becky's achievements. We are a super proud family. It is an important thing to tell you about it as you are part of this story, part of the reason that she chose to become a midwife! My story of how wonderful the midwives were and the empathy they showed to us at such a distressing time had an impact on her and was something that she never forgot. So, although she knew that she would one day work in healthcare, it was partly our experience with you which called to her to go in that direction. If I was looking for some meaning to account for that time, which I stopped a long time ago, this would be it.

Of course, she has first-hand knowledge of how things can actually go wrong, so does not enter her career lightly or thinking that it's all about cuddling babies, as I would have done in her shoes.

I felt that I wanted to write to you to let you know about it, to share how very proud of her we are, and that you also played a major part in all of this. I believe she definitely has the right temperament for this job: very caring but also very practical and level-headed. Becky and her friend set up the first midwives students organisation too. She is amazing, as is your sister Sarah. We are truly blessed.

Last year we managed another family holiday. This time we went to Valencia. I doubt family holidays will continue for much longer as they grow up and want to plan their own trips. I hope they do that and go wherever the mood takes them. Travel is so important as part of lifelong education, I believe, I just wish you had had the opportunity to travel with us too.

I hope that you are looking down on us and smiling at all the things we continue to do. In some small way, we always include you, whether that's a photo or a candle. I do hope that you realise that we will love and miss you until we meet again, one day.

I love you,

Forever and always,

Mummy xxxxxx

Becky the midwife, working in Tanzania.

8th November 2013

My darling Ian,

I wanted to write today as I had another dream about you. It was just so lovely, thank you. It has been a difficult year this year since it is also the year that my dad, your grandad, died after a long illness. It has been one of the toughest years of my life, after the year we lost you.

In this dream there was a beautiful garden on the top of a cliff, with stairs leading down to the beach. The garden was full of my dear departed loved ones, I think they were reassuring me that you are loved. There were so many of them: my dad – your grandad - your nanna - your dad's mum - and so many more, all smiling and looking happy. Then there was you, my darling boy, aged about ten, almost eleven. There you were in your football strip, all white, with a ball, running around excitedly and full of energy and fun. You came to hug me, told me you loved me, then ran off again to play just like most boys of your age would. I cried. I loved seeing you – your dark brown hair, sparkling eyes and a lot like your dad and sisters! It was the most wonderful gift of all

Being able to see you and hold you again, albeit only briefly. All too soon we had to say goodbye. You waved enthusiastically as the garden started to fade and, once again, I told you to come back soon. I woke up my face wet with tears, but I felt warm and fuzzy. The feeling stayed with me all day.

I practice meditation and, during those quiet times, I visualise you too and how I imagine you would look at this time. I do love dreaming about you. The dreams, although not as frequent as I would like, always feel so real. If I was able to, I would make them happen every night, but sadly it really doesn't work like that. When they happen, they are so wonderful and special to me, that I like to lock them away within my heart. So, I write to you to tell you about them so that I can look back as time goes by to remember and relive them once again.

Thank you, my darling boy.

Forever and always,

Mummy xxxxxx

Visitation Dreams Explained

A visitation dream was once explained to me as being very vivid and real; one that you remember for an exceptionally long time afterwards, possibly forever. It should leave you feeling reassured and peaceful, with an overall feeling of being comforted. The dream may give you a very clear message and will make you feel calm and consoled. This feeling will usually be very intense, and you will be able to recall it easily, even several years later. This is unlike our regular dreams, which are easy to forget, where faces are unfamiliar and often forgotten before we even wake. It can be very emotional, but when you wake up from a visitation dream you should be surrounded and comforted by a feeling of love, peace, and gratitude.

According to the spiritual perspective, the appearance of a deceased loved one in our dreams is a sign of love; that they are by our side, watching over us. You will certainly feel reassured and comforted after they visit, even if it is just for a brief moment, but it is often much longer than that and you can carry this feeling around with you for a long time. It is, I feel, a blessing. There were, after all, visitation dreams as far back as the Bible.

I love this analogy and, for me, having experienced these types of dreams, it makes perfect sense. My first visitation dream was from my Nan. We were very close, and it was a long time after her death. It came when I least expected it, but I think when I needed it the most, as with many of these dreams she came to give me some advice, parenting advice. She also imparted information to me to show me that she was aware of what was going on in all of our lives. At the time that this first dream happened, I had no idea what a visitation dream was. It was sometime after I learnt that this is what I had experienced. I realised because I could so easily remember every detail. I still can, and the feeling was one of all-encompassing love.

I then had dreams of Ian, which are recalled here in this book, and finally my dad. My dad and I had had a turbulent relationship and I was not there when he passed, despite regular visits to see him. Some months after he passed, almost a year in fact, he came to offer me comfort and I will always remember his words, *"Don't be sad that you weren't with me when I passed, I was with you when you got the news."*

As I said, these dreams always come when I least expect them. I wish I could conjure them up, but sadly it doesn't work like that. However, whenever I have had a visitation dream, it is always a wonderful experience that leaves me almost with a sense of joy, it is definitely comforting. I do know that not everyone will agree with this, however, this is based on my own experiences, and I share these with you in case you are struggling to understand if something similar has also happened to you or may happen to you in the future. There is also a lot more information that can be found on this topic, but this is a good place to start for a basic explanation and my own personal account.

6th July 2015

My darling Ian,

Thirteen years have passed. You are almost a teenager; how has that happened? I wonder what kind of teenager you would be? Moody maybe? Or would you be unaffected by it all? Your sisters were very different in their teens, and I feel I would have been equipped for pretty much anything.

I had another dream about you! There is no pattern to them, but I am just so grateful when they happen. There you are once more, before my very eyes, again in a white football strip. Is that what they wear in Heaven, I wondered? I opened my arms to you and, although you are almost thirteen, you seemed much younger. You came and sat on my lap and put your arms around my neck; just as you had done in that dream so long ago. I held you for so long, just breathing you in. I asked why you hadn't stayed, and you told me that you couldn't stay, that you had health issues, and that you felt I wouldn't have coped with it. You left me for me. I cried because I told you I wished you would have stayed, to which you replied, "But I am always with you Mum."

I asked how I would know when you were nearby, and you told me, "Look for butterflies and, whenever you see them, know I am near. But I will always be with you mum, don't worry." It was, of course, a wonderful experience, to have the chance to see and be with you again, if only for a brief time.

As lovely as they were, I sometimes doubted my dreams, thinking that it was just my imagination. However, they do come when I haven't been necessarily thinking of you. Then, the very next day, it was as if you knew this was what I was thinking and wanted to let me know that you were always with me as you had said in the dream. Whilst walking to my car after work, as if to allay my fears and show me what you meant, firstly, I saw a car with the number plate 'IAN.' Then, as I continued to walk, two butterflies danced along right in front of me, almost all the way to the car. The final confirmation came as I passed a parked coach on the side of the road. The coach had 'Cygnus' written on the side of it. This, of course, is the name of the star constellation we had named after you! I got the message. Signs are all around us, you just need to be open to seeing them.

If only dreams were real. However, I felt that you had sent me a very clear message this time.

Thank you, my darling boy.

Forever and always,

Mummy xxxxx

Spirituality

Do you ever look up to the skies and smile, saying to yourself, "*I know that was you?*" Or do you sometimes feel the presence of a loved one who has passed? Start humming a tune that reminds you of them even? This, for me, is not only comforting but also spiritual.

The word 'spirituality' can mean different things to different people. Traditionally it was related to one's religious beliefs and faith, and active participation therein and still can mean just that. These days, however, it is a word that encompasses so much more than just that and is also very subjective. It often relates to the meaning of life; how people are connected to each other; truths about the universe; and other mysteries of the human existence. Additionally, it can mean to search for personal growth with non-religious experiences that help you to connect to your spiritual self. For example, through quiet reflection, time in nature, meditation, yoga and seeking to make sense of our lives. Not everyone experiences or expresses spirituality in the same way and, whilst some seek spiritual experiences in all areas of their life, others prefer to be in a spiritual location, like a temple or church. Many people also identify as spiritual but not religious.

Spirituality is very personal, and everyone's path is entirely unique to them. It has been found that spiritual practices can help to lower anxiety and improve self-esteem. Some of the things you can do to start exploring spirituality include paying attention to your feelings. Part of embracing spirituality means encompassing what it means to be human - the good, the bad and the ugly. Focusing on others, empathy and helping others are important aspects of spirituality. Spend time in mediation; some time each morning or evening is ideal, if possible. Mindfulness, becoming more aware of the present, and being less judgemental are also good focuses to have. Practice gratitude and start a journal (I have mentioned this before). This can help to show you what is important to you and identify what brings you joy.

For me, my own religion didn't offer the kind of support I felt I needed after I lost Ian. A priest had visited me in hospital. I found him extremely cold, and he actually got quite annoyed with my questions. I was desperately looking for a reason and answers, there weren't any, but at the time I felt that there must be. I felt he could have had more empathy and understanding. I do not question other people's religion or beliefs, as long as this does not cause harm to others.

12th November 2015

My darling Ian,

It is a very exciting time in our house just now! Becky is getting married to Colin next month! They have been together forever, but they now embark on the next chapter of their life together as husband and wife. There has been a lot of planning and preparation for this big day. We are all just beyond excited. Of course, there's a little bit of stress with all of it too, as you can imagine. Your sister Becky is a perfectionist and wants everything to be perfect, but why shouldn't she; it is a very momentous occasion. At church, in Valletta, I will be escorted down the aisle by a groomsman before Becky enters on the arm of dad. In my heart and mind, you will be with me on this walk, as this would have been a part of your role as a groomsman had you stayed with us. I like to think that you are with us in spirit, as I know Becky does too; we all do. Recently, she asked me if I thought you would have liked Colin. I know beyond any doubt that you would have loved him as the brother that you didn't have. Also, his love of football would have been a huge bond for you both, especially if you supported Italy!

Sarah has been abroad this last year doing her master's degree in Coventry in the UK, an area not too far away from my mum, your nan. She has her graduation just a couple of weeks before the wedding, so you can imagine how busy life is right now. Dad and I will be going over for that. We are so very proud, she already graduated here in Malta and now we are off to celebrate with her this next major achievement in her life. Whilst we're there, we will get to see nan and everyone, then back for the commencement of all the fun things that accompany weddings. We have such a lot going on, but, through it all, my thoughts are not only with them but also with you. The wish that you could be here with us to celebrate is as strong as ever, but I know you'll be here with us in spirit, as always.

We will be spending Christmas and New Year in Birmingham this year; the first time for fifteen years. Becky and Colin will be on their honeymoon; they are going to New Zealand and Australia. Christmas time will be different this year and, of course, I will still light your candle.

I muse on the fact that you would have been a teenager; thirteen years have passed already. I still wonder what kind of teenager would you be? Based on your sisters, it might have been a volatile time for us, however, I have been told that boys are completely different. Sadly, I doubt I will ever know.

I can't help but wonder what or where you would have studied had you been able to stay and, of course, as one of my chicks leaves the nest, who you would have found for your own life partner. This I know will never happen, but it doesn't stop me wondering about what could have been and how different our lives would now be with you in them.

Please watch over us all on this special wedding day and always my love.

Forever and always,

Mummy xxxxxx

Although we cannot see you,

We know you are here

Smiling down

Watching over us

As we say, "I Do"

Forever in our hearts

Forever in our lives

Is where you'll always stay

We will think of you in silence

As we say our vows today.

~ Author Unknown

14th April 2018

My darling Ian,

I have a secret for you. It is so exciting, and I'm sworn to secrecy, but it's okay to tell you...we are going to have a new arrival in the family! Your sister Becky is going to have a baby! Becky and Colin are going to become parents as they welcome their first child, how amazing is that? Baby Mizzi is due in November around my birthday and of course your birthday month too; we have a long time to wait! We won't know what the gender of the baby is, as they want a surprise at the birth. It's such an exciting time for us again, a long-held wish for another baby in the family is being realised. You are going to be an uncle; how cool! I wish you were here to share this special time with us, but I know you are watching over us and looking down on us as the story of our lives continues to grow and change.

Dad and I are off on a holiday soon. We are travelling a lot more these days; it's something I love to do and there are so many places I want to see.

We are going on a Caribbean cruise with Auntie Sheena and Uncle John and afterwards we will spend a few days in Barbados - what a wonderful trip and we will see your nan before we go. We leave with lots of excitement in our hearts. Of course, we are sworn to secrecy for now, but I will let you know when your niece or nephew arrives.

Until then, I am sending all my love to you as always, my darling boy. I love you.

Forever and always

Mummy xxxxx

How to Define a Mother

The definition of motherhood in the dictionary is as follows – '*Motherhood is the state of being a mother. It is the qualities or spirit of a mother. It can also refer to mothers collectively.*'

Mothers come in all shapes and sizes, giving birth to a child is not the only way to become a mother, we see this all the time and all around the world. Babies and children are often times cared for by the extended family, 'surrogate' mothers if you like.

Becoming a mother, whether that is through pregnancy and birth, fostering, adoption, stepchildren, or even just being a stand in mother for someone, are all equally valid, important and involve unconditional love. It is so difficult to define the term 'motherhood' and is more to do with nurturing and loving with all your being, than just having babies. Foster mothers, adoptive mothers, Godmothers and even aunts and sisters can be, and often are, mother figures.

Motherhood is a blessing and birth is a miracle of this I am convinced. It is without doubt, the hardest job I've ever done, and it doesn't come with onsite training or a manual, you're just in the thick of it from the start, it's sink or swim whilst being bombarded with well-meaning advice, often making you feel inadequate, however well intentioned. Constantly second guessing yourself and wondering if you are getting it right. There is also lots of help out there should you need it. Some women find being a mother comes naturally, others not so much. It really doesn't matter how you tackle it, it's always full on.

Although there is progress in sharing the workload between the parents, that comes with babies and children, even now the majority of the burden, for most, falls on the mother. The saying' *it takes a village'* springs to mind.

Sadly, as this book recounts, sometimes there are losses and grief that then becomes a part of your parenting journey. If you have children when you experience this, then you can imagine how things would have been with your baby, based on your already lived experiences and for others it is hard to envision.

Of course, not everyone wants to be a mother or is cut out for the role, and that's absolutely fine, but for those that do it is a lifelong commitment. We are not all the same and that is a good thing, life would be strange if we were all identical, wouldn't it?

Children are not ours to keep, this is true, and motherhood is a blessing and on a more personal note, one of the greatest blessings I have experienced in my life is seeing my baby have a baby of her own.

The natural state of motherhood is unselfishness. When you become a mother, you are no longer the centre of your own universe. You relinquish that position to your children.

Author unknown.

If I were asked to define motherhood, I would have defined it as love in its purest form, unconditional love.

Author unknown.

Being a mother is learning about strengths you didn't know you had and dealing with fears you didn't know existed.

Author unknown.

23rd November 2018

My darling Ian,

Well, you have a niece! She arrived yesterday on my birthday; what a present that was! Dad and I are now grandparents, and I like to think that I am a glamorous grandma! Becky and baby are both doing well and, as you can imagine, we are all just over the moon. It really is so wonderful for me to have a new baby in the family; something I've longed for ever since you left us. Oh, what fun we will have together, the new baby and me. I have already been warned about not spoiling her, but well you know me.

Becky and Colin are soon off to Dublin though at the beginning of next year. Colin has to go to continue with his studying and work. We will go with them to help settle everything and then we will have to visit them on a regular basis, of course. It will be a bit hard initially but it's not forever.

Sarah will also be going to the UK on Boxing Day; it's all happening here! Sarah met a lovely guy called Greg and she is going over to look for a job there and to start a new life with Greg. I hope it works out for her, but please keep an eye on her for me.

And just like that, you are sixteen. Possibly there is no time for you where you are, but it still helps me to imagine how you would look and what you would be doing, I will always measure the years and think fondly of how you would have grown. It's still sometimes painful but it's always nice to think about you now. We will soon be on our own, dad and me. If you were here that would have made life very different for us, but we will also start a new chapter in our lives too. Dad and I are thinking of moving from our house. We have started looking so that we will downsize now that there is just the two of us.

Thinking of you with so much love, as always.

Forever and always

Mummy xxxxxx

Emilia's Poem

Your long curly eyelashes make a shadow on your rosy cheeks,

Your tiny hand curls around my finger, an occasional involuntary twitch,

Golden curls frame your perfect face and your cupid bow lips,

I could stay here all day and watch you as you sleep,

But I know you will soon wake,

I wish that this fleeting moment would last for a while longer,

I take a picture with my mind and store it in my heart,

My gorgeous granddaughter.

Janet Gilson, 2019

6th July 2020

My darling Ian,

Well, eighteen years have passed since we last held you in our arms and said goodbye to you, where has all that time gone? The strangest thing has happened though: we have a global pandemic! It's the scariest thing and we all need to be vaccinated against it! Can you imagine? I had to come back from England earlier than planned, as the airport was going to close. It was really a major inconvenience, and we had no idea how big this thing was or how long it would last, but it doesn't seem to be going anywhere soon. I'm very worried about the situation. It means that I can't see Becky or Sarah and the family, so that's very hard. This is going to be so tough, and I am very worried since I'm classed as vulnerable. I am, of course, very concerned for your nan, but for everyone really. The world is changing so much, and I believe this has been a wakeup call for us all to start taking better care of the planet. We have been warned now for many years even decades, but a lot of people in power have taken little notice. We now have to sit up and pay attention though to protect the planet for all our future generations.

In other more exciting news and onto better things, Sarah and Greg got engaged – during lockdown! How wonderful is that? You know Sarah- she never does anything by halves! I think you would have loved Greg, another football fanatic, so I'm thinking all the boys together would have had a blast. Your dad has his own allies, at last!

This year you would have officially become an adult – eighteen!! I will always wonder what would have been, and how different life would have been for us all as well. I imagine such a handsome young man and really wonder what kind of adult you would have been. Would you be working or studying, and if so, what? As a hobby I'm sure football would have been your thing, at least I strongly suspect it would have been, with all the other influences here, but would there be other things? Dad would have had someone to watch the football with. I always want something else on the TV and, of course, I usually always win. I guess it would have been harder for me to win with two men in the house!

Would you have a special person in your life? So many things to wonder about my darling boy, but you didn't get to stay, and I have accepted that. As I always say though it will never stop me wondering though. Some may say or think that this is unhealthy, but I don't tell them, and I don't care what they think anyway. We all have to live our lives as we deem fit and, for me, that is keeping you a part of my life and our family.

I love you so very much, until next time my darling,

Forever and always

Mummy xxxxx

Empty Nest Syndrome

If you already have children, or if you go on to have children, this time will eventually arise, it comes to us all. It might also bring back thoughts of the child you lost. It did with me when my empty nest syndrome eventually landed. I found myself constantly thinking that if Ian had stayed with us, or indeed if we had been successful in having another child, then I wouldn't be experiencing these feelings just yet. In reality though, you're only delaying the inevitable anyway. It felt as if my empty nest had arrived far too quickly, and for me they both left at around the same time; so definitely not easy. Of course, to help me cope with my feelings, I planned lots of things to keep me distracted from the reality of it all. Eventually though reality catches up with you, it can't be avoided. I did then turn to my gratitude journal, which always helps.

Empty nest syndrome is described as an emotional reaction that may cause feelings of grief, loss, fear, loneliness, sadness and anxiety. In some circumstances it may also lead to depression. It doesn't affect everyone in the same way and is believed to affect women more than men, that doesn't surprise me! It may also lead to marital tensions. I think for me it was more that I had lost my purpose and led me to look for a new meaning in life. I did eventually find that, but I did struggle for a while. There are many things that you can do to counteract these feelings. However, it is important to know that it is very natural to have these feelings, so it's important to feel them and honour them. After all you have been caring for these other humans for all their lives, so it's a very natural response.

It does though give you a chance to renew your own identity and, if part of a couple, to renew your post-child/children relationship. This will now be very different and allow you to pursue each other's interests or find new ones together. You will have more time for each other, and you can make the most of that, if you want to, of course.

It's also been said that empty nest syndrome has been largely over-inflated. However, from experience, I can tell you that this is so real. But, as with everything in life, not everyone will be affected by it in the same way; everyone is different. Some may actually look forward to it since it brings a feeling of freedom from responsibility and a chance to reorganise their lives. Of course, you want your children to grow up and lead their own independent lives, whether that is going away to college/university or just moving out to set up their own homes. It's important to keep the lines of communication open. Explain to them how important they are to you and that you just need to know that they are safe and doing okay. If they then have children of their own, they will eventually realise this.

On a final note, and several years later, I have embraced my empty nest and my new life is wonderful. So, if you're currently going through this, hang on in there. It will get better, and they will be back. They still need you – often more so now, the complexity of their needs just changes.

If you have feelings of depression or anxiety, please seek help.

29th May 2022

My darling Ian,

This month your sister Sarah married Greg here in Malta. It had been postponed due to that blessed pandemic, COVID, which didn't seem to want to leave us. Finally, after many vaccinations and lots of careful planning, we had the wedding, and it was so amazing. It was once again so exciting for all of us and I do wonder about your role. Your sister Sarah had decided that she would walk down the aisle alone, but she did say that she hoped that you would be walking down with her – how marvellous is that! Of course, I was imagining that when she made her grand entrance.

The wedding was very different from Becky and Colin's, but just as beautiful. It was in a garden and the sun shone all day. I thought of you throughout the day, as I always do when we have a major event in the family. I felt your presence, but I didn't feel sad, not anymore. It was such a fabulous day. Becky was Maid of Honour. Emilia, your niece, was flower girl.

It was a really lovely family affair, and we had an absolute ball with friends, old and new You are still often in my thoughts, but just not as strongly as in the beginning. I guess that's normal, and the way things go; how healing happens. I will never forget you though and I carry you everywhere with me in my heart.

Also, you are an uncle again! Becky and Colin welcomed a little boy to the family in February. He is just divine. He is a bigger baby than his sister. She absolutely adores him too and is a great big sister. He is our little Arthur, and he is so cute, I think he will have brown eyes, but only time will tell. We've had a very busy time just lately.

So much has changed since 2002. Our family has grown so much, which, as I'm sure you know, is a delight for me. Two new sons-in-law, who are great and fit in so well with our crazy clan. I now also have two gorgeous grandchildren, who are my entire world. I'm sure you are smiling down on me. As you know, we have a little girl called Emilia and a little boy called Arthur.

I'm not going to lie, when I look at Arthur, I wonder if you would have any similarities. He is very like your sister Sarah in looks, so there's every chance that he would be a little like you, and I love that. Far from making me sad, it makes my heart sing with joy. I finally get a taste of what it's like to have a baby boy in the family and I am looking forward to all his little milestones, just as I have with his sister - my little mini-me. You can now have a conversation with her and it's so lovely. She's so engaging and a little firecracker. How could she not be – born on my birthday?! I really enjoy helping Becky out with them and, of course, it has given me a new lease of life.

Dad was godfather at Arthur's christening, and the godparents get to give a Baptism name to the baby. Dad gave little Arthur your name, Ian. You are always remembered, and I wanted you to know that, he is Arthur James Ian.

Dad and I also moved, back in 2020. Just before the pandemic we found a flat that we loved, and which has an amazing sea view. We have settled in really well and are very happy here.

We kept the other house though. Sarah wanted to leave from there on the day she got married, as it was her family home, and was also where Becky left from on her wedding day. There are so many happy memories there that it was a little sad, but I felt strongly that it was the right thing to do for Dad and me.

Of course, you will be almost twenty now and so grown up. You probably would have constantly complained about me fussing over you, just as your sisters did, but that's just my job as your mum.

I love you Ian,

Forever and always,

Mummy xxxxx

Happiness Abounds – Arthur's Poem

I look around and see all my family staring back at me.

My heart is filled with love and joy,

As I look upon this new little boy

I'm going to hold him close to me for as long as I possibly

can.

Breathe in all those lovely baby smells and cuddle him as

he sleeps,

for I know only too well how fast this time will pass.

Before long he will be grown,

But he'll never outgrow my arms.

Janet Gilson, 2022

Sarah & Greg's Wedding

June 2023

GOODNIGHT, MY DARLING BOY

My darling Ian,

On this, the year that we should have been celebrating your twenty first birthday with you, I wanted to honour you in some small ways throughout the year. A tree will be planted but also, more personally, I wanted to have this book printed for you, in your honour and in memory of you.

Through writing this book and putting it all together, when it was almost complete apart from the final touches, dad and I went away on holiday and took a break from it all- life in general, not just the book. I would, I thought, come back to it with a fresh perspective and new eyes. Of course, I was still thinking about the book while we were away and occasionally, I had an idea and would jot it down to use later when we returned home.

Whilst in Honolulu I ventured into the Christmas shop, (you know me and Christmas) I saw a beautiful ornament for the Christmas tree which I happily thought would be your ornament for this year. I liked the fact that it was from Honolulu. I hoped you would like the book and know that it was for you.

The next day, as I walked along the beach, I found a small white feather. I picked it up and smiled, as I always do, and went to sit on the wall, putting the feather in my bag. Seconds later, another little white feather, just the same, floated down into my lap. I looked around for a bird or a tree – there were none. I smiled again and put it with the other one. Being the person that I am, I said to myself, "Is that you? If so, just send me one more feather so that I'll know for sure." A little while later we set off back to the hotel and there on the floor, further away from where we had been, was another little white feather. I then knew for sure. I appreciate that you are still giving me signs, even after all this time.

I also hope that this book may help other parents who have had to say goodbye to their babies before they even had the chance to get to know them. It is so hard to say goodbye and to realise that this was never meant to be.

Darling, I'm going to end these letters for now. I may still wish to write to you in the future and, if so, then I will continue as and when the mood takes me. But here we are. This book is going to be published for you and me, for your memory. If it helps others, that will be wonderful, won't it?

Always in our hearts, our darling Ian. One day we will all be reunited with each other, and our family chain will once again be complete. There is a piece of my heart that will always, always belong just to you and you alone.

Until we meet again…

I love you,

Forever and always,

Mummy xxxxxx

Feathers from Honolulu

For Ian

The loss of a baby is like no other loss.

It is punctuated with what ifs and maybes.

The pain is just as real, just as valid.

The mourning time, the grieving goes on.

Some may say it's not really the same as losing someone

that you have had in your life longer.

Yes, it is, every loss has an impact.

Every loss has pain and suffering.

All the emptiness of this loss.

The loss of never knowing your baby or the person that

baby would become.

The loss of the joy of new beginnings.

The loss of the warmth of a new baby in your arms.

The loss of hope for that future.

So, don't diminish this loss, it is a great loss just the

same.

Janet Gilson, 2023

Acknowledgements

I would firstly like to thank my family once again for allowing me to share this very personal and painful world we found ourselves in. My daughters Rebecca and Sarah, who lived through this with me and were my constant support and where I found joy when I thought there was none to be found.

To Helen, who has allowed me to portray her role in this story and to all the dedicated midwives and staff in the maternity department of our local hospital who will always have my undying gratitude and respect.

My friends Rita & Paul, who were wonderful and kind helping me through some very difficult times. For allowing their names to be used in this book, Helen, Marcelle, Rita and Paul, Sheena and John. Thanks, from the bottom of my heart to all my wonderful friends who helped to carry me through this untenable situation with their constant love and support.

To Katie, my editor, for her unending patience and my lovely friend Cladonia, for the beautiful book cover. To all mothers, for the reasons I've already stated in this book, but also to parents/siblings and those who have had to endure any life situation like this, may you find comfort.

My lovely, dedicated readers, who continue to support my ramblings and without whom these books would be pointless.

Finally, to Steve, who had to navigate through the situation himself and still continues to hold me up and is always there for me no matter what, my rock.

Twenty-one years have passed and here we are with what I hope is a fitting tribute to my son, Ian. Twenty-one years since I held him. Life continues and there are joys and sorrows in everyday, but the joys outweigh the sorrows, and we must continue to look for the love and happiness all around us.

Whilst writing, old feelings and pain have resurfaced. I am only human, but I am in a good place, and it was certainly cathartic for me. However, if you have been affected by anything in this book, or found any of it triggering, please speak to someone about your feelings, don't suffer in silence, as I did for so much of it. Reach out to your loved ones, or if it's easier, contact one of the organisations below.

Sands – www.sands.org.uk

Stillbirth and neonatal death society

Samaritans – www.samaritans.org

Offering support around the clock if you need to talk to someone.

Space for You

You may have picked up this book because you are going through or have been through similar situations in your own life. Writing these letters to Ian really helped me to feel connected to him, as well as processing the whole situation. As such, I wanted to offer you the opportunity to write your own letters to loved ones on the other side, should you feel drawn to. Use these spaces as you wish; they are yours with love from me to you.

About the Author

Janet Gilson lives in Malta with her husband, and she is both a mother and grandmother. Originally from the UK, she moved to Malta when she met and married her Maltese husband over thirty years ago. She studied psychology and obtained a certificate in counselling, intrigued by how the human mind works and how people recover from trauma. After taking early retirement, she now uses her time doing something she loves – writing. She hopes that by sharing her life experiences, she might help others who have passed through similar experiences. When she's not writing, you will find her spending time with her family, the most important thing in her life. She also loves to travel, believing that this is an education in itself. Janet supports several charities and wants to make a difference, wherever she can. Her previous book is entitled *Behind the Smile,* which can be found on Amazon.

Printed in Great Britain
by Amazon

23831851R00071